Inside the NHL

New Jersey Devils

Taylor Reed

www.av2books.com

AV2 provides enriched content that supplements and complements this book. Weigl's AV2 books strive to create inspired learning and engage young minds in a total learning experience.

Your AV2 Media Enhanced books come alive with...

Audio
Listen to sections of the book read aloud.

Key Words
Study vocabulary, and complete a matching word activity.

Go to **www.av2books.com**, and enter this book's unique code.

Video
Watch informative video clips.

Quizzes
Test your knowledge.

BOOK CODE

X889593

Embedded Weblinks
Gain additional information for research.

Slide Show
View images and captions, and prepare a presentation.

AV2 by Weigl brings you media enhanced books that support active learning.

Try This!
Complete activities and hands-on experiments.

... and much, much more!

Published by AV2 by Weigl
350 5th Avenue, 59th Floor
New York, NY 10118
Websites: www.av2books.com   www.weigl.com

Library of Congress Control Number: 2014951946

ISBN 978-1-4896-3158-9 (hardcover)
ISBN 978-1-4896-3159-6 (single-user eBook)
ISBN 978-1-4896-3160-2 (multi-user eBook)

Printed in the United States of America in Brainerd, Minnesota
1 2 3 4 5 6 7 8 9 0   19 18 17 16 15

032015
WEP050315

Senior Editor Heather Kissock
Art Director Terry Paulhus

Photo Credits
Every reasonable effort has been made to trace ownership and to obtain permission to reprint copyright material. The publishers would be pleased to have any errors or omissions brought to their attention so that they may be corrected in subsequent printings.

Weigl acknowledges Getty Images and iStock as its primary image suppliers for this title.

New Jersey Devils

CONTENTS

Introduction

The New Jersey Devils **franchise** officially began in 1982 when the team moved from Denver, Colorado, to East Rutherford, New Jersey. Formerly known as the Colorado Rockies, the Devils were sold to John McMullen, who promptly moved them east. On October 5, 1982, Don Lever scored the first goal in team history against the Pittsburgh Penguins at the Brendan Byrne Arena. Although that first game ended in a tie, the Devils did plenty of losing that season, scoring just 230 goals, eventually finishing in last place.

Patrik Elias has played 18 NHL seasons, all of them for the New Jersey Devils.

By 1988, the Devils had gained momentum as well as many new fans. They made the **playoffs** for the first time and would go on to the postseason in six of the seven seasons that followed. The Devils had transformed into a winning team, soon to begin a legendary streak that saw them capture three Stanley Cup Championships in just nine years.

In January 2013, the young and talented Travis Zajac signed an eight-year contract to remain in New Jersey through 2020.

New Jersey
DEVILS

Arena Prudential Center

Division Metropolitan

Head Coach Adam Oates and Scott Stevens

Location Newark, New Jersey

NHL Stanley Cup Titles 1995, 2000, 2003

Nicknames Devs, Jersey's team

21
playoff appearances

7
conference finals

9
division champions

3
Stanley Cup championships

History

Martin Brodeur won
691
CAREER VICTORIES
out of a total of 1,266 games
played, both of which
are NHL records.

Martin Brodeur is the
only goalie in NHL history
to record at least 40 wins
in eight seasons.

The inaugural season for the Kansas City Scouts took place in 1974. After two losing campaigns, the brand new NHL team was sold and moved to Denver and renamed the Rockies. The Colorado franchise went on to suffer through six mostly losing seasons. The team was then sold again to successful naval architect, John McMullen, in 1982. McMullen wasted no time in relocating the team to New Jersey. He renamed the team the Devils, based on the legend of the Jersey Devil who roamed the local forests.

Moving the team to Brendan Byrne Arena in East Rutherford was viewed by some as risky business. After all, the well-established New York Islanders and New York Rangers both played within a few miles (kilometers). The Devils quickly transformed into winners, though, and earned a loyal fan base of their own, despite the obstacles. Today, the Devils are one of the most successful franchises in the NHL. Their list of accolades and awards is long, but nothing is as significant as their three Stanley Cup championships.

In their 13th season, the Devils were finally able to hoist the Stanley Cup.

The Arena

More than 600,000 fans showed up to the Prudential Center to watch the Devils play during the 2013–2014 season.

The Prudential Center became the Devils new home in 2007 as part of a $2 billion expansion project for the city of Newark. The plan included the addition of buildings such as Newark Symphony Hall, the Riverfront Stadium, and many restaurants and shops. The center is only two blocks away from Newark Penn Station, which means many fans get to the arena using the train.

One of the main attractions at the Prudential Center is the externally mounted 4,800 square-foot (1,463 square-meter) LED television, one of the largest in the world. The enormous flat screen helps the arena achieve a sleek and modern look. The center has a 17,625-person capacity for hockey games and an 18,500-person limit for basketball when it plays host to the Seton Hall men's basketball team. Prudential Financial bought the **naming rights** to the arena for $105.3 million, an amount to be paid over 20 years.

Perhaps the most unique feature of the arena is located in the lower level grand concourse. Fans congregate here to view historical Devils gear as well as hockey jerseys from New Jersey high schools.

British Columbia
7

Alberta
4
3

CANADA

Saskatchewan

Manitoba
14

Ontario

Washington

Montana

North Dakota

Minnesota
11

Wisconsin
8

Oregon

Idaho

South Dakota

Iowa

Illinois

Wyoming

Nebraska

UNITED STATES

Nevada

6

Utah

Colorado
9

Kansas

Missouri
13

California

5

Arizona
2

New Mexico

Oklahoma

Arkansas

1

Texas
10

Louisiana

Mississ

Pacific Ocean

MEXICO

Gulf of Mexico

WESTERN CONFERENCE
★ ★ ★

PACIFIC DIVISION

1 Anaheim Ducks
2 Arizona Coyotes
3 Calgary Flames
4 Edmonton Oilers

5 Los Angeles Kings
6 San Jose Sharks
7 Vancouver Canucks

CENTRAL DIVISION

8 Chicago Blackhawks
9 Colorado Avalanche
10 Dallas Stars
11 Minnesota Wild

12 Nashville Predators
13 St. Louis Blues
14 Winnipeg Jets

Newfoundland

Quebec

Prince Edward Island

New Brunswick

New Hampshire

20

Vermont

19

Maine

15

Massachusetts

22

26

27

Rhode Island

New York

16

Connecticut

25

Prudential Center, Newark

Michigan

17

Pennsylvania

New Jersey

29

Ohio

Delaware

28

Indiana

24

West Virginia

30

Maryland

Virginia

District of Columbia

Kentucky

23

North Carolina

Tennessee

South Carolina

12

Alabama

Georgia

Atlantic Ocean

ississippi

Florida

21

18

Prudential Center

Arena
Prudential Center

Location
165 Mulberry Street
Newark, New Jersey, 07102

Broke Ground
October 3, 2005

Completed
October 25, 2007

Features
- event rooms that can hold up to 19,000 people
- "farm to fan" food options
- round, glass lobby

LEGEND
☆ Prudential Center
■ Eastern Conference
■ Western Conference

ATLANTIC DIVISION

15 Boston Bruins
16 Buffalo Sabres
17 Detroit Red Wings
18 Florida Panthers
19 Montreal Canadiens
20 Ottawa Senators
21 Tampa Bay Lightning
22 Toronto Maple Leafs

METROPOLITAN DIVISION

23 Carolina Hurricanes
24 Columbus Blue Jackets
★ 25 New Jersey Devils
26 New York Islanders
27 New York Rangers
28 Philadelphia Flyers
29 Pittsburgh Penguins
30 Washington Capitals

NHL EASTERN CONFERENCE

The Uniforms

The Devils have yet to introduce a third jersey, making them one of only two teams in the NHL with only **TWO JERSEYS**. The Detroit Red Wings are the other.

The original Devils' logo was created by the team owner's wife in 1982. It remained on the uniforms for the team's first 10 NHL seasons. In 1992, however, the trim around the logo was changed from green to black.

The Devils' team colors are red, black, and white. They have changed their uniforms a few times to reflect these colors. The most significant uniform change took place in 1992, when they replaced their green pants with black pants. The pants have remained black ever since. The **logo** has also stayed much the same since 1982, with the letters "N" and "J" intertwined, and devil horns evident at the top of the "J."

HOME

AWAY

The players wear either red or white jerseys. The red jerseys have two thin, white stripes surrounding a thicker black stripe on the sleeves and stomach. The white jerseys have the same stripe design, though the thin stripes surrounding the thicker black stripe are red.

The Devils were one of a handful of NHL teams not to make any changes to their uniforms in 2007, when the league adopted a new style of uniform made from high-tech materials.

Helmets and Face Masks

From 1982 to 1992, the Devils wore **RED HELMETS** to match their red road jerseys. Currently, **BLACK HELMETS** are worn with red home jerseys.

The Devils recently participated in the NHL program, Hockey Fights Cancer. They included the program logo on both their home and away helmets.

The Devils helmets are either black or white, depending on whether they are playing at home or away. Considering a goaltender's additional exposure to flying pucks, it is understandable that they need extra protection. Their helmets protect their face as well as their heads and are much larger. Goalies have taken to decorating their helmets in unique ways. This NHL tradition has become nearly as much about art as it is about safety.

Martin Brodeur, one of the greatest goalies of all time, decorated his helmet with pictures of two dogs on it. He named them Stan and Vez, after the Stanley Cup and the Vezina Trophy, which is given out to the best goaltender during a given season. His is a mostly black helmet with the Devils logo on the front. On the sides of the helmet, there is a white strip with red in the middle. The dogs' faces adorn each side of the helmet.

After five years in Vancouver, Cory Schneider became the starting goaltender in New Jersey, putting his creatively designed helmets on full display.

The Coaches

 Before coaching the Devils, Adam Oates guided the Washington Capitals to 65 wins against 45 losses and 17 ties in a season and a half in the United States' capital.

The Devils have had 21 coaches since 1982, and no coach has remained in charge for more than four seasons. Incredibly, when the Devils won three Stanley Cups over a nine-year period, they did so with three different head coaches—Jacques Lemaire, Larry Robinson, and Pat Burns. Jacques Lemaire was hired as the head coach of the Devils on two different occasions, in 1993 and again in 2009.

JACQUES LEMAIRE Jacques Lemaire was a Hall of Fame center for the Montreal Canadiens. He scored 366 goals and racked up 469 **assists** in 853 games over 12 seasons. As the Devils head coach in 1994, he brought a new defensive strategy, the neutral zone trap, with him. This inventive defense focuses on protecting the neutral zone at all costs. It helped the Devils capture their first Stanley Cup Championship.

PAT BURNS Pat Burns had a reputation as a stern taskmaster. This characteristic helped the Devils players right away when he was hired in 2002. Just one year later, the Devils beat the Mighty Ducks of Anaheim to win their third Stanley Cup. Burns is one of two Devils coaches to be inducted into the Hall of Fame.

ADAM OATES AND SCOTT STEVENS After the Devils struggled early in the 2014–2015 season, head coach Peter DeBoer was replaced by a pair of respected hockey men. In a somewhat unheard of move, both Adam Oates and Scott Stevens were named co-head coaches of the Devils. Oates and Stevens are expected to revive a once proud franchise that is only three years removed from playing in the Stanley Cup Final.

Fans and the Internet

Devils fans are loud and proud, holding up signs, chanting, and making the Prudential Center among the best home-ice advantages in the NHL.

The Devils have a popular website, devils.nhl.com, that offers articles about the team, a link to purchase tickets, a team store, and information about the players and coaches. In addition, the site is connected to a social network page that connects fans to Instagram, Twitter, and Facebook. The two most popular team blogs are www.fireandice.northjersey.com, and the more comprehensive www.inlouwetrust.com. Both blogs offer fans a forum to discuss all things Devils.

Fan traditions include chants during games. These chants often occur in concert with the N. J. Devil, who is one of the more beloved **mascots** in the NHL. Some of the chants spell out the team name. One chant is used only when the Devils face their crosstown rival, the Rangers. There is also a chant for the great Martin Brodeur.

Signs
of a fan

#1 Devils fans often pay tribute to former announcer Mike Miller with a chant after each goal.

#2 Fans love the N. J. Devil, the mascot that patrols the Prudential Center, dancing, cheering and firing up fans during home games.

Legends of the Past

Many great players have suited up for the Devils. A few of them have become icons of the team and the city it represents.

Position: Defenseman
NHL Seasons: 20 (1983–2003)
Born: April 17, 1964, in Windsor, Ontario, Canada

Scott Stevens

Stevens was fifth overall pick in the NHL **Entry Draft** in 1982, the same year the Devils moved to New Jersey. He is well known as one of the best defensemen in NHL history. Stevens played eight seasons for the Capitals, one for the Blues, and 13 more with the Devils. He played with all three Devils Stanley Cup teams, and in 1999, he was awarded the Conn Smythe Trophy as the Most Valuable Player (MVP) during the playoffs. Stevens was elected into the Hockey Hall of Fame in 2007. In 2014, Stevens became a co-head coach of the Devils.

Position: Defenseman
NHL Seasons: 22 (1982–2004)
Born: April 1, 1964, in Kitchener, Ontario, Canada

Ken Daneyko

Devils defenseman Ken Daneyko holds the team record for most games played, with 1,283. His 175 playoff games is also a team record. Daneyko was a tough player who punished opponents with big hits. In fact, he logged 2,519 penalty minutes, which is a Devils record that will likely never be broken. Nicknamed "Mr. Devil," Daneyko played each of his 20 seasons for the Devils and helped the team win three Stanley Cups. He was hired in 2014 as a Devils television analyst.

Scott Niedermayer

Skilled defenseman Scott Niedermayer had a true knack for assisting teammates on goals. He played 13 seasons for the Devils, and another five for the Ducks. In his **rookie** season, Niedermayer earned a spot on the NHL All-Rookie Team. Niedermayer has been a winner at every level of hockey. He has won a World Junior Championship, a Memorial Cup, four Stanley Cups, and a World Cup of Hockey gold medal. His jersey is among three numbers that have been retired in Devils' history.

Position: Defenseman
NHL Seasons: 18 (1991–2010)
Born: August 31, 1973, in Edmonton, Alberta, Canada

Martin Brodeur

Simply put, Martin Brodeur may be the greatest goalie ever. He is the NHL's all-time leader in regular season wins, **shutouts**, and games played. Brodeur is a five-time winner of the William M. Jennings trophy, an award that is given to the most talented goaltender in a season. He is also a nine-time **All-Star** and a Calder Memorial Trophy winner, as the rookie of the year. Brodeur was known for his puck handling and quick reflexes, which helped him achieve a .912 **save percentage** over his 22-year NHL career.

Position: Goaltender
NHL Seasons: 22 (1992–2015)
Born: May 6, 1972, in Montreal, Quebec, Canada

Stars of Today

Today's Devs team is made up of many young, talented players who have proven that they are among the best in the league.

Position: Left Wing
NHL Seasons: 19 (1994–Present)
Born: April 13, 1976, in Trebic, Czechoslovakia

Patrik Elias

Patrik Elias holds the Devils' team records for most goals, most points, and most game-winning goals. Elias has played for the Devils for his entire 17-year NHL career. During that time, he has rightly earned the nickname "Mr. Overtime" due to his special talent for game-winning shots and assists during extra time. Elias was a part of Devils Stanley Cup championship teams in 1999 and 2002, but his greatest season came in 2000 when he recorded 96 points, an all-time team record.

Travis Zajac

Travis Zajac was the 20th overall selection by the Devils in the 2004 NHL Entry Draft. In 2008, Zajac became the Devils' first **line** center, winning 52.4 percent of his face-offs while playing alongside Zach Parise and Jamie Langenbrunner. He began that season as the least celebrated of the star-studded line, known as "ZZ Pop," but he soon became a fan favorite. Zajac is a versatile player, able to score on the **power play** as well stop a power play on the defensive end. He became an especially important part of the Devils' plans during the 2013 season, when Zach Parise left to sign with the Minnesota Wild.

Position: Center
NHL Seasons: 9 (2006–Present)
Born: May 13, 1985, in Winnipeg, Manitoba, Canada

Cory Schneider

After five years in Vancouver, Cory Schneider arrived in New Jersey in 2013 with some very large shoes to fill. The 2013 season was his first as starting goaltender for the Devils. Schneider replaced legendary Martin Brodeur between the pipes. During his first season with the Devils, Schneider had a .921 save percentage and a 1.97 **goals against average**, which ranked him third best in the NHL. He recently signed a seven-year contract with the Devils that will keep him in New Jersey through the 2021–2022 season.

Position: Goaltender
NHL Seasons: 8 (2007–Present)
Born: March 18, 1986, in Marblehead, Massachusetts, United States

All-Time Records

1,283
Most Games Played
Ken Daneyko holds the record for most games played as a Devil. He played in a total of 1,283 games.

60
Most Assists
Scott Stevens had 60 assists during the 1993–1994 season. He also scored the most points as a defenseman in that same year, with 78 points.

393
Most Goals
Patrik Elias has scored the most goals as a Devil, with 393 at the end of the 2013–2014 season, while John MacLean and Bobby Holik follow him with 347 and 202 goals respectively.

12
Most Shutouts
Martin Brodeur had 12 shutouts during the 2006–2007 season. He had 10 or more shutouts in four seasons.

401
Longest Iron Man Streak
Travis Zajac accomplished the feat of playing in 401 straight games, the longest such streak in team history.

Timeline

Throughout the team's history, the Devils have had many memorable events that have become defining moments for the team and its fans.

1982
The Devils franchise begins its inaugural season in East Rutherford, New Jersey, after new owner John McMullen moves the franchise out of Denver.

1995
The Devils win their first Stanley Cup under the leadership of Head Coach Jacques Lemaire. This is the first of three Stanley Cups the Devils will win over a nine-year period.

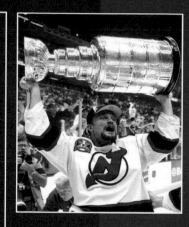

| 1980 | 1984 | 1988 | 1992 | 1996 | 2000 |

1983
The Devils are defeated by the Edmonton Oilers as all-time great, Wayne Gretzky, complains that the Devils are playing a "Mickey Mouse" game, by not putting quality players out on the ice. This starts the tradition of Oilers fans wearing Mickey Mouse ears at Devils games.

In 1999, Ken Daneyko plays his 1,000th game as a Devil in a win against the Carolina Hurricanes. Daneyko becomes the first player in franchise history to reach this historic mark.

The Future

The Devils have been a winning franchise for much of their storied history in New Jersey. They played in the Stanley Cup Final five times, winning three Cups. In doing so, they have captured much of the fan base in the tri-state area, despite heavy competition from the Rangers and Islanders. With a new star goalie tending the net and a core group of young stars playing in a strong defensive system, there will no doubt be more winning seasons ahead.

2000

The Devils face the Dallas Stars in the Stanley Cup Final, beating them in six games. The final win is a double-overtime thriller, earning the Devils their second Stanley Cup Championship.

An agreement is made between Newark and the Devils for a new arena, which would later become known as the Prudential Center. In October 2005, construction on the new arena begins.

2001 — **2004** — **2007** — **2010** — **2013** — **2016**

2003

The Devils win their third Stanley Cup Championship, beating the Mighty Ducks of Anaheim in seven games. Martin Brodeur records three shutouts during the final.

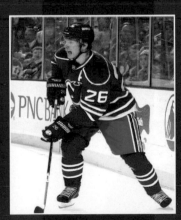

2010

During a game against the Penguins, the Devils wear green for the first time since 1992.

2013

The Prudential Center hosts the NHL Entry Draft, marking the first time an arena in the metropolitan New York area has hosted the draft.

Write a Biography

Life Story

A person's life story can be the subject of a book. This kind of book is called a biography. Biographies often describe the lives of people who have achieved great success. These people may be alive today, or they may have lived many years ago. Reading a biography can help you learn more about a great person.

Get the Facts

Use this book, and research in the library and on the internet, to find out more about your favorite Devil. Learn as much about this player as you can. What position does he play? What are his statistics in important categories? Has he set any records? Also, be sure to write down key events in the person's life. What was his childhood like? What has he accomplished off the field? Is there anything else that makes this person special or unusual?

Use the Concept Web

A concept web is a useful research tool. Read the questions in the concept web on the following page. Answer the questions in your notebook. Your answers will help you write a biography.

Concept Web

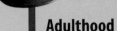

Adulthood
- Where does this individual currently reside?
- Does he or she have a family?

Your Opinion
- What did you learn from the books you read in your research?
- Would you suggest these books to others?
- Was anything missing from these books?

Childhood
- Where and when was this person born?
- Describe his or her parents, siblings, and friends.
- Did this person grow up in unusual circumstances?

Accomplishments off the Field
- What is this person's life's work?
- Has he or she received awards or recognition for accomplishments?
- How have this person's accomplishments served others?

Write a Biography

Help and Obstacles
- Did this individual have a positive attitude?
- Did he or she receive help from others?
- Did this person have a mentor?
- Did this person face any hardships?
- If so, how were the hardships overcome?

Accomplishments on the Field
- What records does this person hold?
- What key games and plays have defined his career?
- What are his stats in categories important to his position?

Work and Preparation
- What was this person's education?
- What was his or her work experience?
- How does this person work?
- What is the process he or she uses?

Trivia Time

Take this quiz to test your knowledge of the New Jersey Devils. The answers are printed upside down under each question.

1 What was the name of the Devils' first arena?

A. The Brendan Byrne Arena

2 What was the name of the Colorado franchise before the team was moved to New Jersey?

A. Colorado Rockies

3 How many Stanley Cup championships have the Devils won?

A. Three

4 Who holds the record for most games played?

A. Ken Daneyko

5 Which player holds the record for most goals?

A. Patrik Elias

6 Who are the current coaches of the New Jersey Devils?

A. Adam Oates and Scott Stevens

7 Which ex-Devils coach was inducted into the Hockey Hall of Fame in 1984?

A. Jacques Lemaire

8 How many head coaches have the New Jersey Devils employed?

A. 21

9 Which goalie decorated his helmet with dogs named Vez and Stan?

A. Martin Brodeur

Key Words

All-Star: a game made for the best-ranked players in the NHL that happens mid-season. A player can be named an All-Star and then be sent to play in this game.

assists: a statistic that is attributed to up to two players of the scoring team who shoot, pass, or deflect the puck toward the scoring teammate

entry draft: an annual meeting where different teams in the NHL are allowed to pick new, young players who can join their teams

franchise: a team that is a member of a professional sports league

goals against average: a statistic that is the average of goals allowed per game by a goaltender

line: forwards who play in a group, or "shift," during a game

logo: a symbol that stands for a team or organization

mascots: characters, usually animals, that are chosen to represent teams

naming rights: a form of advertisement for a company or another business who pays to have its name advertised at the forefront of an NHL arena

playoffs: a series of games that occur after regular season play

power play: when a player from one team is in the penalty box, the other team gains an advantage in the number of players

rookie: a player age 26 or younger who has played no more than 25 games in a previous season, nor six or more games in two previous seasons

save percentage: the rate at which a goalie stops shots being made toward his net by the opposing team

shutouts: a game in which the losing team is blocked from making any goals

Index

Log on to www.av2books.com

AV² by Weigl brings you media enhanced books that support active learning. Go to www.av2books.com, and enter the special code found on page 2 of this book. You will gain access to enriched and enhanced content that supplements and complements this book. Content includes video, audio, weblinks, quizzes, a slide show, and activities.

AV² Online Navigation

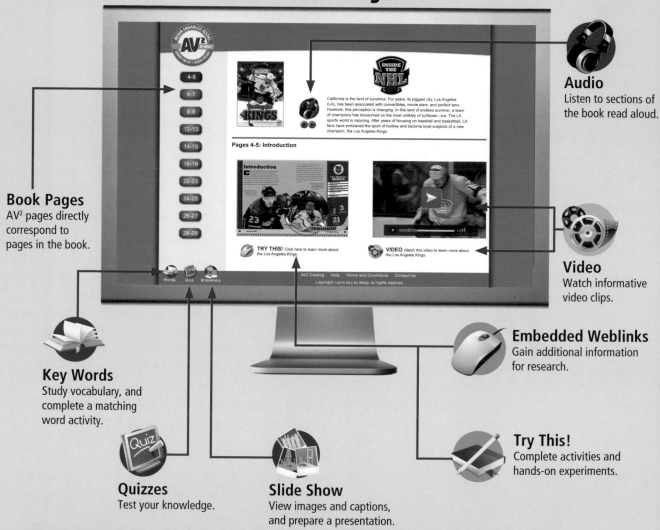

Audio
Listen to sections of the book read aloud.

Book Pages
AV² pages directly correspond to pages in the book.

Video
Watch informative video clips.

Embedded Weblinks
Gain additional information for research.

Key Words
Study vocabulary, and complete a matching word activity.

Try This!
Complete activities and hands-on experiments.

Quizzes
Test your knowledge.

Slide Show
View images and captions, and prepare a presentation.

AV² was built to bridge the gap between print and digital. We encourage you to tell us what you like and what you want to see in the future.

Sign up to be an AV² Ambassador at www.av2books.com/ambassador.